BIG BOOK of VOLUNTEER APPRECIATION IDEAS

Your willingness brings JOY to a great JOY as

Thanks

THANKS

PROMISES,

by Joyce Tepfer

Gospel Light

HOW TO MAKE CLEAN COPIES FROM THIS BOOK

You may make copies of portions of this book with a clean conscience if

- you (or someone in your organization) are the original purchaser;

- you are using the copies you make for a noncommercial purpose (such as teaching or promoting your ministry) within your church or organization;

- you follow the instructions provided in this book.

However, it is ILLEGAL for you to make copies if

- you are using the material to promote, advertise or sell a product or service other than for ministry fund-raising;

- you are using the material in or on a product for sale; or

- you or your organization are not the original purchaser of this book.

By following these guidelines you help us keep our products affordable.

Thank you,

Gospel Light

Editorial Staff

Founder, Dr. Henrietta Mears

Publisher Emeritus, William T. Greig

Senior Consulting Publisher, Dr. Elmer L. Towns

Senior Managing Editor, Sheryl Haystead

Senior Consulting Editor, Wesley Haystead, M.S.Ed.

Senior Editor, Biblical and Theological Issues, Bayard Taylor, M.Div.

Editorial Team, Mary Gross Davis, Karen McGraw

Contributing Editors, Michelle Anthony, Debbie Barber, Rachel Hong, Arlonne Monroe

Art Directors, Lenndy McCullough, Christina Renée Sharp, Samantha A. Hsu

Designer, Zelle Olson

Scripture quotations are taken from the *Holy Bible, New International Version*®. Copyright © 1973, 1978, 1984 by International Bible Society. Used by permission of Zondervan Publishing House. All rights reserved.

The views and opinions expressed by the author in this book do not represent those of the companies whose products are mentioned. The use of any trademarked name does not indicate that the owner of that trademark endorses in any way the material in this book.

Contents

CANDY

*Your willingness to serve and be a role model for our kids brings **JOY** to our hearts. We're asking God to give you great **JOY** as you love the kids He brings!*

*Some Children's Ministry volunteers may never get public applause or recognition from the pulpit. They may never know what a **grand-slam** difference they have made. But to us, you're more famous than **BABE RUTH**!*

***BAR NONE**—You're the best! Your willingness to give your best to the children at our church is GREATLY APPRECIATED!*

***SAVE** your **BREATH** along with your strength and energy! We'll need you back next week for your fabulous input on the team!*

*Thank you for honoring God, the keeper of **PROMISES**, with your gift of service. Future servants are watching you to learn how to do it!*

*You don't have to be a **SQUARE** to work in Children's Ministry, but it helps to have the corner on **love, patience, time** and **prayer**. Thanks for sharing these priceless gifts so generously!*

*Your faithful service is like **gold** to us! Your ministry is a **nugget** of blessing for our entire church. Thank you!*

*Your love for Jesus and children has been like finding **gold** for us! Keep giving out those **nuggets** of biblical principle through your life and words.*

*No amount of **gold** could replace the great value you bring to our kids through your love and care. Thank you!*

*Thanks for being such a priceless **nugget**! We struck **real gold** when we found you for the Children's Ministry team!*

*You are one of the **golden treasures** of Children's Ministry. We value you highly!*

*Thanks for helping us to **strike gold** in our Children's Ministry. You have laid up some valuable treasure in heaven!*

*It can be a **CRUNCH** to be faithful when we hear: "**C**hildren's Ministry takes too much work!" "**R**ights to adult fellowship time come FIRST!" "**U**rgent personal matters need most of my attention." "**N**ot interrupting MY sleep to arrive early!" "**C**ommitment? I don't feel like it today." "**H**ow much more time will this take?" Your faithful, cheerful help takes a **bite** out of the **CRUNCH**! THANK YOU!*

*Here's **100 GRAND** to show our **rich** appreciation—even though you're worth more than any amount of money to our Children's Ministry!*

*Thanks for being one of the great leaders on our Children's Ministry team. You are a **TREASURE** to us!*

*Thanks for sharing the **TREASURES** of God's love with our kids. We value you!*

*Thanking you **NOW and LATER**! **Now** you are blessing our kids through our Children's Ministry. **Later** you will receive heavenly rewards for your investment!*

***PAYDAY** for your unselfish investment with children here on Earth will come when you are richly rewarded at the **Bank of Heaven**! We're all blessed by the dividends of your investment in our precious "loans from God" here at our family branch. Thanks!*

***PAYDAY** in heaven will be seeing the results of what God has done through your faithful service with kids. Thanks for doing what you do so faithfully!*

*People often say that kids and **peanut butter** go hand in hand. But we know it's YOU—going hand in hand with kids and parents—who makes the spiritual nurturing of our precious kids possible. THANKS!*

*Your creative teaching and faithful service make you one **RED HOT** teacher! Thank you!*

*What a **SMARTIE** you are to choose to be part of our Children's Ministry team! We appreciate you!*

*Others would **SNICKER**, if only they knew how much fun they could have in Kids' Ministry, too! Spread the **snickers**! Encourage a friend to join you in serving Jesus through leading His kids!*

*We're about to **BURST** with excitement at the influence you're having in Children's Ministry! Thanks for shining like a **STAR** with the love of Jesus!*

*Your efforts for our children are truly **SWEET**! Thanks for doing your best for each child.*

***T**eachers **W**ield **I**ndelible e**X**amples. Thanks for letting God use your example before our children. You are noticed!*

DRINKS

FOOD

Thanks for bringing your gifts to our Children's Ministry **COMBO**. Your contribution is helping make a great beat and some spicy harmony!

Your contribution to our Children's Ministry **COMBO** has added variety, color and great flavor. Thanks for cooking up some great moments this year!

If Children's Ministry were a box of **CRACKER JACK**, you'd be the **prize** in our box! Thanks for being such a winner with our kids.

Our Savior is the Son of **DAVID** and the Son of God! Thank you for sowing the **seeds** of the age-old message in new ways to produce eternal results!

Thanks for faithfully putting one **FOOT** in front of the other in Children's Ministry. God will multiply every **inch** of your progress into **miles** of spiritual understanding for our kids!

Just as shepherds in the **fields** watched their flocks by night—so you have wonderfully watched kids by night (and day) in our church **fields**. Please enjoy this treat from **MRS. FIELDS**—you're outstanding in your **field**!

As you enjoy your **OREO** cereal, remember that you're **O**bviously, **R**eally, **E**specially **O**utstanding in our Children's Ministry!

O for Outstanding / **R** for Reliable / **E** for Enthusiastic / **O** for One of a Kind / These only begin to describe the many unique qualities you bring to our Children's Ministry team. You are greatly appreciated!

Thank you for the **O**utstanding **R**elational and **E**ducational **O**ffering you make. People are learning from you every week!

You don't have to be **nuts** to lead kids, but it helps—to be **nuts** about kids, that is! And you are! Thanks for all the great ways you share God's love with them!

Thank you for **raisin'** the standard in our Children's Ministry by your faithful service and love for our kids.

You add so much to our Children's Ministry! Thank you for being the **salt** of the earth and **rounding** out our team!

God **mustard** had you in mind when we planned our children's program this year—because you've done a marvelous job of **spicing** it up and smothering kids with His love! Thank you—and enjoy!

GUM

*Thanks for your faithful help! Such faithfulness keeps the programs in our ministry from getting all **gummed up**! (And we're delighted to see how creatively you **stick** with it!)*

*Thanks for being such a **cool** addition to our Children's Ministry team. No matter how **hot** a situation becomes, your **warm** heart toward each kid is noticed by God and appreciated by others. As you reflect on your contribution, we thought **ICE** might be nice!*

HOUSEHOLD ITEMS

*We're **banding** together for the spiritual **aid** of our kids. Thanks for bringing a **soft** heart for children and a **flexible** attitude that **protects** those in your care! We love and appreciate you!*

*Our special thanks to our leaders, teachers and helpers who just keep **going and going and going**! You **energize** every part of Children's Ministry with your faithfulness!*

*Thank you for your commitment to sharing the **Book of books** with the children of our church—the leaders of tomorrow!*

*Thanks for being one more **light** on the path connecting kids with the real meaning of Christmas! May God bless and enrich your holiday season!*

*Thanks for choosing to help **smooth out** the rough edges in our Children's Ministry. Your helpful presence **shapes** many young lives!*

*Celebrating with you the coming of Jesus, the **Light of the world**. We're delighted to see how His **light** shines through you to bless our kids!*

*Your involvement in Children's Ministry gives new meaning to "Got it **covered**!" Thanks for **covering** your God-given assignment with faithfulness, prayer and joy! We appreciate all you do!*

*Softer hands that smell good, too, / Is what this product does for you! / As you rub this lotion on, / Ask God for a heart that's **soft** and **strong**. Thank Him for His promises, too— / And for the love He'll show through you!*

*We love the way your presence in our program **smoothes out the wrinkles** in our Children's Ministry. Thanks for being **soft** and **flexible**! You are appreciated!*

*We're glad to see how God's love comes through you to our little ones! Children's Ministry takes work—even getting your hands **dirty**. But you are making a difference. Thank you for sharing your service and His love!*

*Thanks for **hanging around** with our kids so that your love for our Lord is right where they can see it. Keep **hanging** close to Him. You are appreciated!*

*If it weren't for volunteers like you, we'd be **clean** out of wonderful Children's Ministry leaders! Thanks for your **clean**-cut example that teaches so many!*

*Thank you for being a great example of a servant. You have demonstrated Christlike service to many who watch you. May this small token encourage you as you continue to **serve** the Lord with gladness!*

*We can see that God's grace has given you **extra strength** to meet the needs of our kids! We pray you will remain **extra resistant** to the enemy's distractions and as **gentle** as a PUFF toward each child's needs.*

*Recipe for Effective Children's Ministry at Our Church / **Ingredients:** YOU! / God's Word / A bunch of kids / A plan of action / **Directions:** Thoroughly mix ingredients together with time and prayer. Bake at temperatures well warmed by love, keeping an eye on how God changes the children's lives. Garnish with laughter and serve to the King as a special gift of love at Christmas.*

*Let's be like sponges this year! **Soft** and **flexible** in our hearts / **Saturated** by freely **absorbing** God's Word / Living **clean** in light of His forgiveness / **Oozing** His love when **squeezed** by the press of life. / We appreciate you!*

*When you swish this little washcloth over your hands, we'd like for you to remember how your help and encouragement have **refreshed** our entire Children's Ministry staff this year. Thank you!*

MISCELLANEOUS

*On the first Christmas, **angels** sang to praise God for Jesus' birth. This Christmas, we think you're an **angel**, too. Thank you for sharing God's love with our children!*

*We can see you've **absorbed** God's light by the way your life **reflects** His. Thanks for being like a **star** to our children, showing them the way to Jesus. We appreciate you!*

*May you be enriched by knowing the **key** role you play in the lives of impressionable children. You are being used to **unlock** God's message of love as children share with you their ideas, thoughts and feelings. Thank you!*

Look! It's the place where YOU make a difference! Thank you for serving the Lord on our Children's Ministry team!

*Thank you for your **smile** and your ministry that will point kids to Jesus. We're glad you've chosen to **stick** with it!*

OFFICE SUPPLIES

*What's in a **name**? A child's own **name** is the most important word in his or her vocabulary! Thank you for remembering each child's **name** and for giving the individual attention that makes God's amazing love real to a child. We appreciate you!*

*Make no mistake about it—God knew yesterday that you'd be here today, making a difference in kids' lives forever! **Erase** any doubt about your mission! His plan, implemented by your love, is making a difference. Thank you!*

*Your participation has been a **highlight** in Children's Ministry this year! Thank you!*

*We love the way you **hold things together** and keep everyone **connected**! Thank you for your joyful service in our Children's Ministry!*

*Your ministry with kids is **write on**! Know that you are loved and appreciated.*

*Thanks for **sticking** with us to the end. Your participation has been **noteworthy**!*

*Thanks for **sticking** with us through this dynamic season in Children's Ministry. Unlike temporary adhesive, your example, relationships and words will **adhere** to young hearts and minds for eternity!*

*Your nimble fingers keep our Children's Ministry on the **cutting edge**. Thank you very much for all you do!*

PHOTOS

*What do the **ABCs** of Children's Ministry look like at our church? **A**BLE / **B**EAUTIFUL / **C**OMMITTED / **D**YNAMIC / **E**NERGETIC / **F**AITHFUL / **G**REAT—and more! THANK YOU!*

When there's a job to be done, you look for a team LIKE THIS! You are the best! We're grateful for you!

*This year's **picture** of Children's Ministry would have been incomplete without you! Thank you for being **clearly focused** on our great God!*

Index

How to Use This Book

Whether a church is small, medium-sized or huge, the importance of volunteers is indisputable! There could never be enough paid staff members to teach every class, prepare every curriculum piece and play with the toddlers, too! Volunteers in children's ministry freely share their time, love and talents in a variety of unique ways to serve, nourish and bless the next generation of the Church.

A volunteer's personal touch and individual attention help lay the foundation of biblical knowledge while providing children with a living example of what a Christian looks like, acts like and sounds like. The writer of Hebrews tells us to "spur one another toward love and good deeds [and to] encourage one another" (Hebrews 10:24-25). And as anyone who's been a children's ministry volunteer can tell you, even the most faithful of us can use a boost now and then!

That's the purpose for this book: to provide quick and doable ways for children's ministry directors to encourage, thank and lovingly spur on those faithful volunteers who change children's ministry plans into programs that produce spiritual fruit in the lives of children!

Your Encouragement Kit

To most efficiently use this book, keep these items at hand:

- Colored copier paper or card stock

- Paper cutter (or fancy-edged scissors)

- Hole punch

- Curling ribbon

- Scissors

- Tape

- Seasonal stickers

Step-by-Step Guidelines

1. Select, remove and photocopy the desired page. (Remember to return the page to the book!) Cut off the top portion from the photocopy and then position this page in the copier as your master. (To make more copies at once, prepare two pages as masters. Then copy them side by side onto 11x17-inch [28-cmx43-cm] paper.)

2. Use a paper cutter (or scissors) to separate the message cards. Attach cards to items in any of the ways illustrated below.

3. Add a personal message or seasonal stickers if desired. Your unique creative touch increases the value of each gift!

4. Use these gifts with a message in a variety of ways:

  • Remembrance gifts (birthdays, holidays, anniversary of years in ministry, etc.)

  • Surprise gifts placed in each classroom

  • Favors or place cards at an appreciation tea, luncheon or other event

  • Encouragement gifts (placed on each chair at a training meeting or handed to each volunteer at a volunteer dedication service)

Candy

Your willingness to serve and be a role model for our kids brings **JOY** to our hearts. We're asking God to give you great **JOY** as you love the kids He brings!

Your willingness to serve and be a role model for our kids brings **JOY** to our hearts. We're asking God to give you great **JOY** as you love the kids He brings!

Your willingness to serve and be a role model for our kids brings **JOY** to our hearts. We're asking God to give you great **JOY** as you love the kids He brings!

Your willingness to serve and be a role model for our kids brings **JOY** to our hearts. We're asking God to give you great **JOY** as you love the kids He brings!

Candy

Some Children's Ministry volunteers may never get public applause or recognition from the pulpit. They may never know what a **grand-slam** difference they have made. But to us, you're more famous than BABE RUTH!

Some Children's Ministry volunteers may never get public applause or recognition from the pulpit. They may never know what a **grand-slam** difference they have made. But to us, you're more famous than BABE RUTH!

Some Children's Ministry volunteers may never get public applause or recognition from the pulpit. They may never know what a **grand-slam** difference they have made. But to us, you're more famous than BABE RUTH!

Some Children's Ministry volunteers may never get public applause or recognition from the pulpit. They may never know what a **grand-slam** difference they have made. But to us, you're more famous than BABE RUTH!

Candy

Your willingness to give your best to the children at our church is

GREATLY APPRECIATED!

Your willingness to give your best to the children at our church is

GREATLY APPRECIATED!

Your willingness to give your best to the children at our church is

GREATLY APPRECIATED!

Your willingness to give your best to the children at our church is

GREATLY APPRECIATED!

Candy

SAVE your BREATH

along with your strength and energy! We'll need you back next week for your fabulous input on the team!

SAVE your BREATH

along with your strength and energy! We'll need you back next week for your fabulous input on the team!

SAVE your BREATH

along with your strength and energy! We'll need you back next week for your fabulous input on the team!

SAVE your BREATH

along with your strength and energy! We'll need you back next week for your fabulous input on the team!

Candy

Thank you
for honoring God,
the keeper of

PROMISES,

with your gift of
service. Future servants
are watching you to learn
how to do it!

Thank you
for honoring God,
the keeper of

PROMISES,

with your gift of
service. Future servants
are watching you to learn
how to do it!

Thank you
for honoring God,
the keeper of

PROMISES,

with your gift of
service. Future servants
are watching you to learn
how to do it!

Thank you
for honoring God,
the keeper of

PROMISES,

with your gift of
service. Future servants
are watching you to learn
how to do it!

**Ghirardelli®
Chocolate Squares Candies**

Candy

You don't have to be a **SQUARE** to work in Children's Ministry,

but it helps to have the corner on

love, patience, time and prayer.

Thanks for sharing these priceless gifts so generously!

You don't have to be a **SQUARE** to work in Children's Ministry,

but it helps to have the corner on

love, patience, time and prayer.

Thanks for sharing these priceless gifts so generously!

You don't have to be a **SQUARE** to work in Children's Ministry,

but it helps to have the corner on

love, patience, time and prayer.

Thanks for sharing these priceless gifts so generously!

You don't have to be a **SQUARE** to work in Children's Ministry,

but it helps to have the corner on

love, patience, time and prayer.

Thanks for sharing these priceless gifts so generously!

Candy

Your faithful service is like **gold** to us!
Your ministry is a **nugget** of blessing for our entire church.
Thank you!

Your faithful service is like **gold** to us!
Your ministry is a **nugget** of blessing for our entire church.
Thank you!

Your faithful service is like **gold** to us!
Your ministry is a **nugget** of blessing for our entire church.
Thank you!

Your faithful service is like **gold** to us!
Your ministry is a **nugget** of blessing for our entire church.
Thank you!

Candy

Your love for Jesus and children has been like finding **gold** for us! Keep giving out those **nuggets** of biblical principle through your life and words.

Your love for Jesus and children has been like finding **gold** for us! Keep giving out those **nuggets** of biblical principle through your life and words.

Your love for Jesus and children has been like finding **gold** for us! Keep giving out those **nuggets** of biblical principle through your life and words.

Your love for Jesus and children has been like finding **gold** for us! Keep giving out those **nuggets** of biblical principle through your life and words.

Candy

No amount of **gold** could replace the great value you bring to our kids through your love and care.

Thank you!

No amount of **gold** could replace the great value you bring to our kids through your love and care.

Thank you!

No amount of **gold** could replace the great value you bring to our kids through your love and care.

Thank you!

No amount of **gold** could replace the great value you bring to our kids through your love and care.

Thank you!

No amount of **gold** could replace the great value you bring to our kids through your love and care.

Thank you!

No amount of **gold** could replace the great value you bring to our kids through your love and care.

Thank you!

Gold Foil-Wrapped Candies

Candy

Thanks for Being such a Priceless nugget!

24 KT.

We struck **real gold** when we found you for the Children's Ministry team!

Thanks for Being such a Priceless nugget!

24 KT.

We struck **real gold** when we found you for the Children's Ministry team!

Thanks for Being such a Priceless nugget!

24 KT.

We struck **real gold** when we found you for the Children's Ministry team!

Thanks for Being such a Priceless nugget!

24 KT.

We struck **real gold** when we found you for the Children's Ministry team!

Thanks for Being such a Priceless nugget!

24 KT.

We struck **real gold** when we found you for the Children's Ministry team!

Candy

You are one of the
golden treasures
of Children's Ministry. We value you highly!

You are one of the
golden treasures
of Children's Ministry. We value you highly!

You are one of the
golden treasures
of Children's Ministry. We value you highly!

You are one of the
golden treasures
of Children's Ministry. We value you highly!

**Gold Foil-Wrapped
Peanut Butter Cups**

Candy

THANKS for helping us to strike gold in our Children's Ministry. You have laid up some valuable treasure in heaven!

THANKS for helping us to strike gold in our Children's Ministry. You have laid up some valuable treasure in heaven!

THANKS for helping us to strike gold in our Children's Ministry. You have laid up some valuable treasure in heaven!

THANKS for helping us to strike gold in our Children's Ministry. You have laid up some valuable treasure in heaven!

THANKS for helping us to strike gold in our Children's Ministry. You have laid up some valuable treasure in heaven!

THANKS for helping us to strike gold in our Children's Ministry. You have laid up some valuable treasure in heaven!

Candy

You are a
CLASSIC
example of a
godly servant,
faithfully loving
our precious kids.
We appreciate the
way you unwrap
God's love
for our kids.
Thanks!

You are a
CLASSIC
example of a
godly servant,
faithfully loving
our precious kids.
We appreciate the
way you unwrap
God's love
for our kids.
Thanks!

You are a
CLASSIC
example of a
godly servant,
faithfully loving
our precious kids.
We appreciate the
way you unwrap
God's love
for our kids.
Thanks!

You are a
CLASSIC
example of a
godly servant,
faithfully loving
our precious kids.
We appreciate the
way you unwrap
God's love
for our kids.
Thanks!

Candy

These sweet little HUGS come your way to say,
"We couldn't have made it without your teamwork!
Thank you for your wonderful help!"

These sweet little HUGS come your way to say,
"We couldn't have made it without your teamwork!
Thank you for your wonderful help!"

These sweet little HUGS come your way to say,
"We couldn't have made it without your teamwork!
Thank you for your wonderful help!"

Candy

Like these **jellybeans**, your time with our children this Easter added bright color and fresh **flavor** to the telling of God's **sweetest** story of love.
Thanks for helping to make the true meaning so clear!

Like these **jellybeans**, your time with our children this Easter added bright color and fresh **flavor** to the telling of God's **sweetest** story of love.
Thanks for helping to make the true meaning so clear!

Like these **jellybeans**, your time with our children this Easter added bright color and fresh **flavor** to the telling of God's **sweetest** story of love.
Thanks for helping to make the true meaning so clear!

Candy

We love to see
Children's Ministry
team members as
Jolly
as you are!
Thank you for the cheerful
way you express your love
for God and kids as you
work with our young ones
(even when it might feel
like you're
rounding up
a herd)!

We love to see
Children's Ministry
team members as
Jolly
as you are!
Thank you for the cheerful
way you express your love
for God and kids as you
work with our young ones
(even when it might feel
like you're
rounding up
a herd)!

We love to see
Children's Ministry
team members as
Jolly
as you are!
Thank you for the cheerful
way you express your love
for God and kids as you
work with our young ones
(even when it might feel
like you're
rounding up
a herd)!

We love to see
Children's Ministry
team members as
Jolly
as you are!
Thank you for the cheerful
way you express your love
for God and kids as you
work with our young ones
(even when it might feel
like you're
rounding up
a herd)!

Candy

Thanks
for helping our kids
discover a **MINT** of
valuable truth from God's
Word! We love the way
you keep your **COOL** and
keep them motivated!

Thanks
for helping our kids
discover a **MINT** of
valuable truth from God's
Word! We love the way
you keep your **COOL** and
keep them motivated!

Thanks
for helping our kids
discover a **MINT** of
valuable truth from God's
Word! We love the way
you keep your **COOL** and
keep them motivated!

Thanks
for helping our kids
discover a **MINT** of
valuable truth from God's
Word! We love the way
you keep your **COOL** and
keep them motivated!

Candy

Candy

LifeSavers® Candies
(assorted flavors)

Candy

Thank you!

Substitutes
are great—they **save** the day!

Thank you!

Substitutes
are great—they **save** the day!

Thank you!

Substitutes
are great—they **save** the day!

Thank you!

Substitutes
are great—they **save** the day!

Candy

You bring unique **flavor** to our Children's Ministry team.

Thanks for doing your part!

You bring unique **flavor** to our Children's Ministry team.

Thanks for doing your part!

You bring unique **flavor** to our Children's Ministry team.

Thanks for doing your part!

You bring unique **flavor** to our Children's Ministry team.

Thanks for doing your part!

Candy

You have been a

LIFESAVER
by responding to our need for a substitute! May God bless you richly for your service.

You have been a

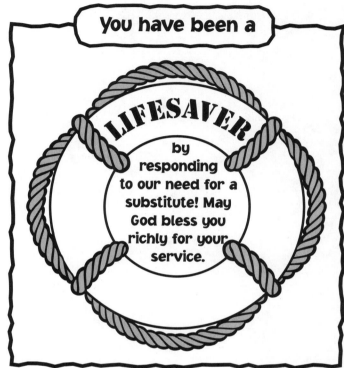

LIFESAVER
by responding to our need for a substitute! May God bless you richly for your service.

You have been a

LIFESAVER
by responding to our need for a substitute! May God bless you richly for your service.

You have been a

LIFESAVER
by responding to our need for a substitute! May God bless you richly for your service.

Candy

Candy

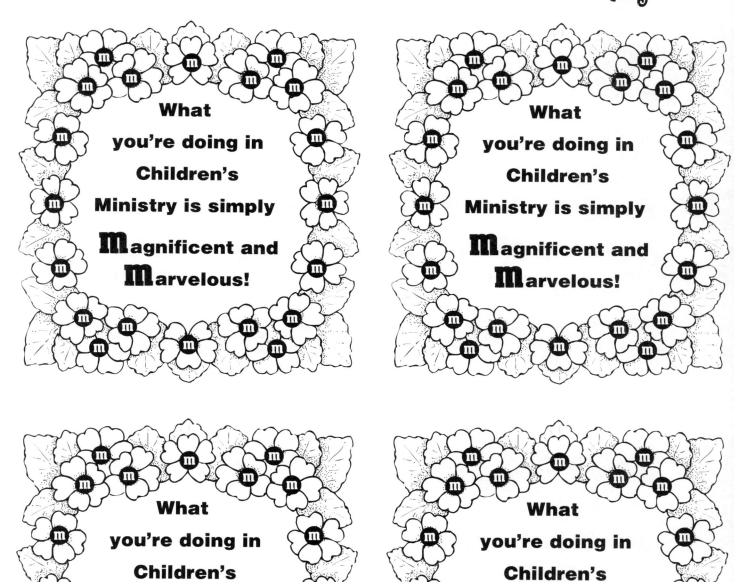

What you're doing in Children's Ministry is simply Magnificent and Marvelous!

What you're doing in Children's Ministry is simply Magnificent and Marvelous!

What you're doing in Children's Ministry is simply Magnificent and Marvelous!

What you're doing in Children's Ministry is simply Magnificent and Marvelous!

Candy

Your ministry to children is Magnificent and Meaningful.
It Magnifies the King and Makes a difference for eternity.

Thank you!

Your ministry to children is Magnificent and Meaningful.
It Magnifies the King and Makes a difference for eternity.

Thank you!

Your ministry to children is Magnificent and Meaningful.
It Magnifies the King and Makes a difference for eternity.

Thank you!

Candy

We got a **mint** of great potential when we picked you to lead kids in our program. You're **cool** under pressure and full of creative ideas! Thank you for being a great example of Jesus' love!

We got a **mint** of great potential when we picked you to lead kids in our program. You're **cool** under pressure and full of creative ideas! Thank you for being a great example of Jesus' love!

We got a **mint** of great potential when we picked you to lead kids in our program. You're **cool** under pressure and full of creative ideas! Thank you for being a great example of Jesus' love!

We got a **mint** of great potential when we picked you to lead kids in our program. You're **cool** under pressure and full of creative ideas! Thank you for being a great example of Jesus' love!

Mounds® Candy Bars

Candy

MOUNDS
of appreciation for the very vital role
you play in our Children's Ministry! Your significant contribution blesses our entire church family.

MOUNDS
of appreciation for the very vital role
you play in our Children's Ministry! Your significant contribution blesses our entire church family.

MOUNDS
of appreciation for the very vital role
you play in our Children's Ministry! Your significant contribution blesses our entire church family.

MOUNDS
of appreciation for the very vital role
you play in our Children's Ministry! Your significant contribution blesses our entire church family.

Candy

It can be a CRUNCH to be faithful when we hear:

"**C**hildren's Ministry takes too much work!"
"**R**ights to adult fellowship time come FIRST!"
"**U**rgent personal matters need most of my attention."
"**N**ot interrupting MY sleep to arrive early!"
"**C**ommitment? I don't feel like it today."
"**H**ow much more time will this take?"

Your faithful, cheerful help takes a **bite**
out of the CRUNCH! THANK YOU!

It can be a CRUNCH to be faithful when we hear:

"**C**hildren's Ministry takes too much work!"
"**R**ights to adult fellowship time come FIRST!"
"**U**rgent personal matters need most of my attention."
"**N**ot interrupting MY sleep to arrive early!"
"**C**ommitment? I don't feel like it today."
"**H**ow much more time will this take?"

Your faithful, cheerful help takes a **bite**
out of the CRUNCH! THANK YOU!

It can be a CRUNCH to be faithful when we hear:

"**C**hildren's Ministry takes too much work!"
"**R**ights to adult fellowship time come FIRST!"
"**U**rgent personal matters need most of my attention."
"**N**ot interrupting MY sleep to arrive early!"
"**C**ommitment? I don't feel like it today."
"**H**ow much more time will this take?"

Your faithful, cheerful help takes a **bite**
out of the CRUNCH! THANK YOU!

Candy

Here's

100 GRAND

to show our **rich** appreciation—even though you're worth more than any amount of money to our Children's Ministry!

Here's

100 GRAND

to show our **rich** appreciation—even though you're worth more than any amount of money to our Children's Ministry!

Here's

100 GRAND

to show our **rich** appreciation—even though you're worth more than any amount of money to our Children's Ministry!

Here's

100 GRAND

to show our **rich** appreciation—even though you're worth more than any amount of money to our Children's Ministry!

Candy

Thanks
for being one of the great
leaders on our Children's
Ministry team.
You are a TREASURE to us!

Thanks
for being one of the great
leaders on our Children's
Ministry team.
You are a TREASURE to us!

Thanks
for being one of the great
leaders on our Children's
Ministry team.
You are a TREASURE to us!

Thanks
for being one of the great
leaders on our Children's
Ministry team.
You are a TREASURE to us!

Thanks
for being one of the great
leaders on our Children's
Ministry team.
You are a TREASURE to us!

Thanks
for being one of the great
leaders on our Children's
Ministry team.
You are a TREASURE to us!

Candy

Thanks for sharing the TREASURES
of God's love with our kids.

We value you!

Thanks for sharing the TREASURES
of God's love with our kids.

We value you!

Thanks for sharing the TREASURES
of God's love with our kids.

We value you!

Candy

Thanking you
NOW and LATER!

Now
you are blessing our kids through our Children's Ministry.

Later
you will receive heavenly rewards for your investment!

Thanking you
NOW and LATER!

Now
you are blessing our kids through our Children's Ministry.

Later
you will receive heavenly rewards for your investment!

Thanking you
NOW and LATER!

Now
you are blessing our kids through our Children's Ministry.

Later
you will receive heavenly rewards for your investment!

Thanking you
NOW and LATER!

Now
you are blessing our kids through our Children's Ministry.

Later
you will receive heavenly rewards for your investment!

Candy

PAYDAY

for your unselfish investment with children here on Earth will come when you are richly rewarded at the **Bank of Heaven**! We're all blessed by the dividends of your investment in our precious "loans from God" here at our family branch. Thanks!

PAYDAY

for your unselfish investment with children here on Earth will come when you are richly rewarded at the **Bank of Heaven**! We're all blessed by the dividends of your investment in our precious "loans from God" here at our family branch. Thanks!

PAYDAY

for your unselfish investment with children here on Earth will come when you are richly rewarded at the **Bank of Heaven**! We're all blessed by the dividends of your investment in our precious "loans from God" here at our family branch. Thanks!

PAYDAY

for your unselfish investment with children here on Earth will come when you are richly rewarded at the **Bank of Heaven**! We're all blessed by the dividends of your investment in our precious "loans from God" here at our family branch. Thanks!

Candy

PAYDAY in heaven will be seeing the results of what God has done through your faithful service with kids. **Thanks for doing what you do so faithfully!**

PAYDAY in heaven will be seeing the results of what God has done through your faithful service with kids. **Thanks for doing what you do so faithfully!**

PAYDAY in heaven will be seeing the results of what God has done through your faithful service with kids. **Thanks for doing what you do so faithfully!**

PAYDAY in heaven will be seeing the results of what God has done through your faithful service with kids. **Thanks for doing what you do so faithfully!**

Candy

People often say that kids and **peanut butter** go hand in hand. But we know it's YOU—going hand in hand with kids and parents—who makes the spiritual nurturing of our precious kids possible. **THANKS!**

People often say that kids and **peanut butter** go hand in hand. But we know it's YOU—going hand in hand with kids and parents—who makes the spiritual nurturing of our precious kids possible. **THANKS!**

People often say that kids and **peanut butter** go hand in hand. But we know it's YOU—going hand in hand with kids and parents—who makes the spiritual nurturing of our precious kids possible. **THANKS!**

People often say that kids and **peanut butter** go hand in hand. But we know it's YOU—going hand in hand with kids and parents—who makes the spiritual nurturing of our precious kids possible. **THANKS!**

Candy

Your creative teaching and faithful service make you one

RED HOT teacher!

Thank you!

Your creative teaching and faithful service make you one

RED HOT teacher!

Thank you!

Your creative teaching and faithful service make you one

RED HOT teacher!

Thank you!

Your creative teaching and faithful service make you one

RED HOT teacher!

Thank you!

Candy

What a **SMARTIE** you are to choose to be part of our Children's Ministry team! We appreciate you!

What a **SMARTIE** you are to choose to be part of our Children's Ministry team! We appreciate you!

What a **SMARTIE** you are to choose to be part of our Children's Ministry team! We appreciate you!

What a **SMARTIE** you are to choose to be part of our Children's Ministry team! We appreciate you!

What a **SMARTIE** you are to choose to be part of our Children's Ministry team! We appreciate you!

What a **SMARTIE** you are to choose to be part of our Children's Ministry team! We appreciate you!

Candy

Others would
SNICKER,
if only they knew
how much fun they
could have in Kids'
Ministry, too!
Spread the snickers!
Encourage a friend to
join you in serving
Jesus through
leading His kids!

Others would
SNICKER,
if only they knew
how much fun they
could have in Kids'
Ministry, too!
Spread the snickers!
Encourage a friend to
join you in serving
Jesus through
leading His kids!

Others would
SNICKER,
if only they knew
how much fun they
could have in Kids'
Ministry, too!
Spread the snickers!
Encourage a friend to
join you in serving
Jesus through
leading His kids!

Others would
SNICKER,
if only they knew
how much fun they
could have in Kids'
Ministry, too!
Spread the snickers!
Encourage a friend to
join you in serving
Jesus through
leading His kids!

Candy

We're about to **BURST** with excitement at the influence you're having in Children's Ministry! Thanks for shining like a **STAR** with the love of Jesus!

We're about to **BURST** with excitement at the influence you're having in Children's Ministry! Thanks for shining like a **STAR** with the love of Jesus!

We're about to **BURST** with excitement at the influence you're having in Children's Ministry! Thanks for shining like a **STAR** with the love of Jesus!

We're about to **BURST** with excitement at the influence you're having in Children's Ministry! Thanks for shining like a **STAR** with the love of Jesus!

Candy

Your efforts for our
children are truly SWEET!
Thanks for doing your best for each child.

Your efforts for our
children are truly SWEET!
Thanks for doing your best for each child.

Your efforts for our
children are truly SWEET!
Thanks for doing your best for each child.

Candy

Teachers Wield Indelible eXamples.

THANKS FOR LETTING GOD USE YOUR EXAMPLE BEFORE OUR CHILDREN.

YOU ARE NOTICED!

Teachers Wield Indelible eXamples.

THANKS FOR LETTING GOD USE YOUR EXAMPLE BEFORE OUR CHILDREN.

YOU ARE NOTICED!

Teachers Wield Indelible eXamples.

THANKS FOR LETTING GOD USE YOUR EXAMPLE BEFORE OUR CHILDREN.

YOU ARE NOTICED!

Teachers Wield Indelible eXamples.

THANKS FOR LETTING GOD USE YOUR EXAMPLE BEFORE OUR CHILDREN.

YOU ARE NOTICED!

Candy

In Children's Ministry, it helps to be a
TWIZZLER:

Teachable
Wise
Interested
Zany
Zealous
Loving Jesus
Energetic
Real

God appreciates the flavor you bring
to what you do—and so do we!

Thank you!

In Children's Ministry, it helps to be a
TWIZZLER:

Teachable
Wise
Interested
Zany
Zealous
Loving Jesus
Energetic
Real

God appreciates the flavor you bring
to what you do—and so do we!

Thank you!

In Children's Ministry, it helps to be a
TWIZZLER:

Teachable
Wise
Interested
Zany
Zealous
Loving Jesus
Energetic
Real

God appreciates the flavor you bring
to what you do—and so do we!

Thank you!

In Children's Ministry, it helps to be a
TWIZZLER:

Teachable
Wise
Interested
Zany
Zealous
Loving Jesus
Energetic
Real

God appreciates the flavor you bring
to what you do—and so do we!

Thank you!

Candy

WE THANK GOD FOR
A SERVANT LIKE
YOU—WILLING TO BE A
WHOPPER
OF AN INFLUENCE TO
THE NEXT GENERATION
AS YOU LEAD THEM
TOWARD OUR
GREAT GOD!

WE THANK GOD FOR
A SERVANT LIKE
YOU—WILLING TO BE A
WHOPPER
OF AN INFLUENCE TO
THE NEXT GENERATION
AS YOU LEAD THEM
TOWARD OUR
GREAT GOD!

WE THANK GOD FOR
A SERVANT LIKE
YOU—WILLING TO BE A
WHOPPER
OF AN INFLUENCE TO
THE NEXT GENERATION
AS YOU LEAD THEM
TOWARD OUR
GREAT GOD!

WE THANK GOD FOR
A SERVANT LIKE
YOU—WILLING TO BE A
WHOPPER
OF AN INFLUENCE TO
THE NEXT GENERATION
AS YOU LEAD THEM
TOWARD OUR
GREAT GOD!

Drinks

ORANGE YOU GLAD YOU'RE IN CHILDREN'S MINISTRY? DON'T YOU WISH EVERYONE WAS?

ORANGE YOU GLAD YOU'RE IN CHILDREN'S MINISTRY? DON'T YOU WISH EVERYONE WAS?

ORANGE YOU GLAD YOU'RE IN CHILDREN'S MINISTRY? DON'T YOU WISH EVERYONE WAS?

ORANGE YOU GLAD YOU'RE IN CHILDREN'S MINISTRY? DON'T YOU WISH EVERYONE WAS?

ORANGE YOU GLAD YOU'RE IN CHILDREN'S MINISTRY? DON'T YOU WISH EVERYONE WAS?

ORANGE YOU GLAD YOU'RE IN CHILDREN'S MINISTRY? DON'T YOU WISH EVERYONE WAS?

ORANGE YOU GLAD YOU'RE IN CHILDREN'S MINISTRY? DON'T YOU WISH EVERYONE WAS?

ORANGE YOU GLAD YOU'RE IN CHILDREN'S MINISTRY? DON'T YOU WISH EVERYONE WAS?

Drinks

Thanks for giving a **SLICE** of your time and yourself to influence our children toward our loving God.

Thanks for giving a **SLICE** of your time and yourself to influence our children toward our loving God.

Thanks for giving a **SLICE** of your time and yourself to influence our children toward our loving God.

Thanks for giving a **SLICE** of your time and yourself to influence our children toward our loving God.

Thanks for giving a **SLICE** of your time and yourself to influence our children toward our loving God.

Thanks for giving a **SLICE** of your time and yourself to influence our children toward our loving God.

Thanks for being a **classic** example of a loving servant. We appreciate your joyful help in communicating the **classic** and lasting truths of God's Word to our kids!

Thanks for being a **classic** example of a loving servant. We appreciate your joyful help in communicating the **classic** and lasting truths of God's Word to our kids!

Thanks for being a **classic** example of a loving servant. We appreciate your joyful help in communicating the **classic** and lasting truths of God's Word to our kids!

Thanks for being a **classic** example of a loving servant. We appreciate your joyful help in communicating the **classic** and lasting truths of God's Word to our kids!

Drinks

This describes you to a **T**:

**Terrific
Trustworthy
Tenacious
Tireless**

Now enjoy a cup of tea while you reflect on all you've seen God do through you and around you!

This describes you to a **T**:

**Terrific
Trustworthy
Tenacious
Tireless**

Now enjoy a cup of tea while you reflect on all you've seen God do through you and around you!

This describes you to a **T**:

**Terrific
Trustworthy
Tenacious
Tireless**

Now enjoy a cup of tea while you reflect on all you've seen God do through you and around you!

This describes you to a **T**:

**Terrific
Trustworthy
Tenacious
Tireless**

Now enjoy a cup of tea while you reflect on all you've seen God do through you and around you!

Drinks

Merry Christmas

to a very important member of our Children's Ministry team! Thanks for being a faithful **PIPELINE** to the source of **LIVING WATER**.

Merry Christmas

to a very important member of our Children's Ministry team! Thanks for being a faithful **PIPELINE** to the source of **LIVING WATER**.

Food

It's absolutely true:
Because of all you do,
Our team (without you)
Would feel like a crazy zoo!
(We might go
CRACKERS
without your help!)

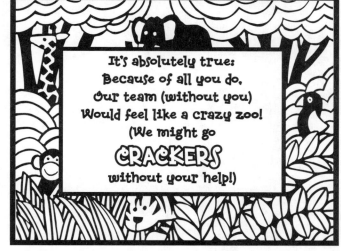

It's absolutely true:
Because of all you do,
Our team (without you)
Would feel like a crazy zoo!
(We might go
CRACKERS
without your help!)

It's absolutely true:
Because of all you do,
Our team (without you)
Would feel like a crazy zoo!
(We might go
CRACKERS
without your help!)

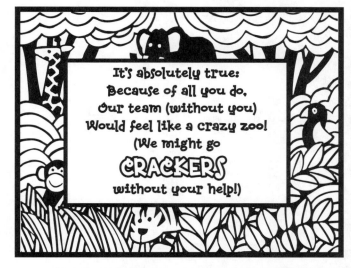

It's absolutely true:
Because of all you do,
Our team (without you)
Would feel like a crazy zoo!
(We might go
CRACKERS
without your help!)

It's absolutely true:
Because of all you do,
Our team (without you)
Would feel like a crazy zoo!
(We might go
CRACKERS
without your help!)

It's absolutely true:
Because of all you do,
Our team (without you)
Would feel like a crazy zoo!
(We might go
CRACKERS
without your help!)

Food

We appreciate the fresh and flavorful help you're giving in our Children's Ministry!

You're the **APPLE** of God's eye!

We appreciate the fresh and flavorful help you're giving in our Children's Ministry!

You're the **APPLE** of God's eye!

We appreciate the fresh and flavorful help you're giving in our Children's Ministry!

You're the **APPLE** of God's eye!

We appreciate the fresh and flavorful help you're giving in our Children's Ministry!

You're the **APPLE** of God's eye!

Food

If our Children's Ministry team were a cookie, you'd be the chocolate chips!
Thanks for adding so much to our ministry!

If our Children's Ministry team were a cookie, you'd be the chocolate chips!
Thanks for adding so much to our ministry!

If our Children's Ministry team were a cookie, you'd be the chocolate chips!
Thanks for adding so much to our ministry!

If our Children's Ministry team were a cookie, you'd be the chocolate chips!
Thanks for adding so much to our ministry!

Food

Wise men with gifts, shepherds with sheep,

Telling the words of a story to keep.

Angels with tidings of wonderful news—

All celebrated the King of the Jews.

We're thankful for you; knowing you is a treat.

Your love for our children makes our joy complete!

Merry Christmas!

Wise men with gifts, shepherds with sheep,

Telling the words of a story to keep.

Angels with tidings of wonderful news—

All celebrated the King of the Jews.

We're thankful for you; knowing you is a treat.

Your love for our children makes our joy complete!

Merry Christmas!

Wise men with gifts, shepherds with sheep,

Telling the words of a story to keep.

Angels with tidings of wonderful news—

All celebrated the King of the Jews.

We're thankful for you; knowing you is a treat.

Your love for our children makes our joy complete!

Merry Christmas!

Wise men with gifts, shepherds with sheep,

Telling the words of a story to keep.

Angels with tidings of wonderful news—

All celebrated the King of the Jews.

We're thankful for you; knowing you is a treat.

Your love for our children makes our joy complete!

Merry Christmas!

Food

Thanks for Bringing your Gifts to our Children's Ministry **COMBO**. Your Contribution is helping make a Great Beat and some Spicy harmony!

Thanks for Bringing your Gifts to our Children's Ministry **COMBO**. Your Contribution is helping make a Great Beat and some Spicy harmony!

Thanks for Bringing your Gifts to our Children's Ministry **COMBO**. Your Contribution is helping make a Great Beat and some Spicy harmony!

Thanks for Bringing your Gifts to our Children's Ministry **COMBO**. Your Contribution is helping make a Great Beat and some Spicy harmony!

Food

YOUR CONTRIBUTION
TO OUR CHILDREN'S
MINISTRY
COMBO
HAS ADDED VARIETY,
COLOR AND
GREAT FLAVOR.
THANKS FOR
COOKING UP
SOME GREAT
MOMENTS
THIS YEAR!

YOUR CONTRIBUTION
TO OUR CHILDREN'S
MINISTRY
COMBO
HAS ADDED VARIETY,
COLOR AND
GREAT FLAVOR.
THANKS FOR
COOKING UP
SOME GREAT
MOMENTS
THIS YEAR!

YOUR CONTRIBUTION
TO OUR CHILDREN'S
MINISTRY
COMBO
HAS ADDED VARIETY,
COLOR AND
GREAT FLAVOR.
THANKS FOR
COOKING UP
SOME GREAT
MOMENTS
THIS YEAR!

YOUR CONTRIBUTION
TO OUR CHILDREN'S
MINISTRY
COMBO
HAS ADDED VARIETY,
COLOR AND
GREAT FLAVOR.
THANKS FOR
COOKING UP
SOME GREAT
MOMENTS
THIS YEAR!

If Children's Ministry were a box of **CRACKER JACK**, you'd be the **prize** in our box! Thanks for being such a winner with our kids.

If Children's Ministry were a box of **CRACKER JACK**, you'd be the **prize** in our box! Thanks for being such a winner with our kids.

If Children's Ministry were a box of **CRACKER JACK**, you'd be the **prize** in our box! Thanks for being such a winner with our kids.

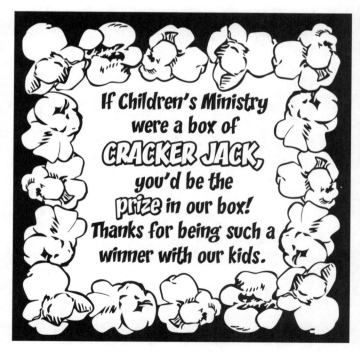

If Children's Ministry were a box of **CRACKER JACK**, you'd be the **prize** in our box! Thanks for being such a winner with our kids.

Food

Our Savior is the Son of DAVID and the Son of God! Thank you for sowing the seeds of the age-old message in new ways to produce eternal results!

Our Savior is the Son of DAVID and the Son of God! Thank you for sowing the seeds of the age-old message in new ways to produce eternal results!

Our Savior is the Son of DAVID and the Son of God! Thank you for sowing the seeds of the age-old message in new ways to produce eternal results!

Our Savior is the Son of DAVID and the Son of God! Thank you for sowing the seeds of the age-old message in new ways to produce eternal results!

Food

Thanks for faithfully putting one **FOOT** in front of the other in Children's Ministry. God will multiply every **inch** of your progress into **miles** of spiritual understanding for our kids!

Thanks for faithfully putting one **FOOT** in front of the other in Children's Ministry. God will multiply every **inch** of your progress into **miles** of spiritual understanding for our kids!

Thanks for faithfully putting one **FOOT** in front of the other in Children's Ministry. God will multiply every **inch** of your progress into **miles** of spiritual understanding for our kids!

Food

Just as shepherds in the fields watched their flocks by night—so you have wonderfully watched kids by night (and day) in our church fields. Please enjoy this treat from **MRS. FIELDS**—you're outstanding in your field!

Just as shepherds in the fields watched their flocks by night—so you have wonderfully watched kids by night (and day) in our church fields. Please enjoy this treat from **MRS. FIELDS**—you're outstanding in your field!

Just as shepherds in the fields watched their flocks by night—so you have wonderfully watched kids by night (and day) in our church fields. Please enjoy this treat from **MRS. FIELDS**—you're outstanding in your field!

Food

As you enjoy your OREO cereal, remember that you're

Obviously,
Really,
Especially
Outstanding

in our Children's Ministry!

As you enjoy your OREO cereal, remember that you're

Obviously,
Really,
Especially
Outstanding

in our Children's Ministry!

As you enjoy your OREO cereal, remember that you're

Obviously,
Really,
Especially
Outstanding

in our Children's Ministry!

As you enjoy your OREO cereal, remember that you're

Obviously,
Really,
Especially
Outstanding

in our Children's Ministry!

Food

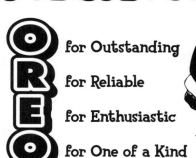

O for Outstanding

R for Reliable

E for Enthusiastic

O for One of a Kind

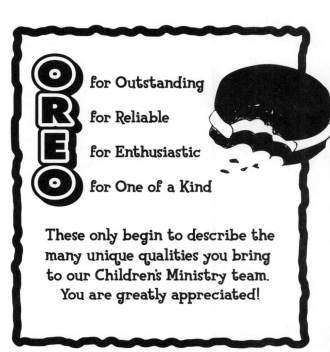

These only begin to describe the
many unique qualities you bring
to our Children's Ministry team.
You are greatly appreciated!

O for Outstanding

R for Reliable

E for Enthusiastic

O for One of a Kind

These only begin to describe the
many unique qualities you bring
to our Children's Ministry team.
You are greatly appreciated!

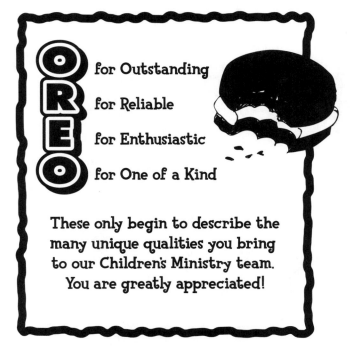

O for Outstanding

R for Reliable

E for Enthusiastic

O for One of a Kind

These only begin to describe the
many unique qualities you bring
to our Children's Ministry team.
You are greatly appreciated!

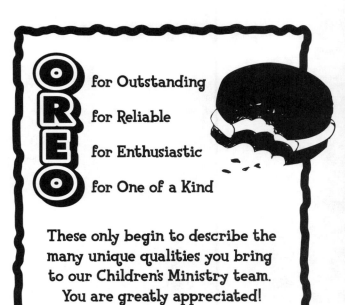

O for Outstanding

R for Reliable

E for Enthusiastic

O for One of a Kind

These only begin to describe the
many unique qualities you bring
to our Children's Ministry team.
You are greatly appreciated!

Food

THANK YOU FOR THE

Outstanding

Relational and

Educational

Offering you make.

PEOPLE ARE LEARNING FROM YOU EVERY WEEK!

THANK YOU FOR THE

Outstanding

Relational and

Educational

Offering you make.

PEOPLE ARE LEARNING FROM YOU EVERY WEEK!

THANK YOU FOR THE

Outstanding

Relational and

Educational

Offering you make.

PEOPLE ARE LEARNING FROM YOU EVERY WEEK!

THANK YOU FOR THE

Outstanding

Relational and

Educational

Offering you make.

PEOPLE ARE LEARNING FROM YOU EVERY WEEK!

Food

You don't have to be **nuts** to lead kids, but it helps-to be **nuts** about kids, that is! And you are! Thanks for all the great ways you share God's love with them!

You don't have to be **nuts** to lead kids, but it helps-to be **nuts** about kids, that is! And you are! Thanks for all the great ways you share God's love with them!

You don't have to be **nuts** to lead kids, but it helps-to be **nuts** about kids, that is! And you are! Thanks for all the great ways you share God's love with them!

Raisins (miniature boxes)

Food

 THANK YOU FOR **RAISIN'** THE STANDARD IN OUR CHILDREN'S MINISTRY BY YOUR FAITHFUL SERVICE AND LOVE FOR OUR KIDS.

 THANK YOU FOR **RAISIN'** THE STANDARD IN OUR CHILDREN'S MINISTRY BY YOUR FAITHFUL SERVICE AND LOVE FOR OUR KIDS.

 THANK YOU FOR **RAISIN'** THE STANDARD IN OUR CHILDREN'S MINISTRY BY YOUR FAITHFUL SERVICE AND LOVE FOR OUR KIDS.

 THANK YOU FOR **RAISIN'** THE STANDARD IN OUR CHILDREN'S MINISTRY BY YOUR FAITHFUL SERVICE AND LOVE FOR OUR KIDS.

 THANK YOU FOR **RAISIN'** THE STANDARD IN OUR CHILDREN'S MINISTRY BY YOUR FAITHFUL SERVICE AND LOVE FOR OUR KIDS.

 THANK YOU FOR **RAISIN'** THE STANDARD IN OUR CHILDREN'S MINISTRY BY YOUR FAITHFUL SERVICE AND LOVE FOR OUR KIDS.

 THANK YOU FOR **RAISIN'** THE STANDARD IN OUR CHILDREN'S MINISTRY BY YOUR FAITHFUL SERVICE AND LOVE FOR OUR KIDS.

 THANK YOU FOR **RAISIN'** THE STANDARD IN OUR CHILDREN'S MINISTRY BY YOUR FAITHFUL SERVICE AND LOVE FOR OUR KIDS.

 THANK YOU FOR **RAISIN'** THE STANDARD IN OUR CHILDREN'S MINISTRY BY YOUR FAITHFUL SERVICE AND LOVE FOR OUR KIDS.

 THANK YOU FOR **RAISIN'** THE STANDARD IN OUR CHILDREN'S MINISTRY BY YOUR FAITHFUL SERVICE AND LOVE FOR OUR KIDS.

 THANK YOU FOR **RAISIN'** THE STANDARD IN OUR CHILDREN'S MINISTRY BY YOUR FAITHFUL SERVICE AND LOVE FOR OUR KIDS.

 THANK YOU FOR **RAISIN'** THE STANDARD IN OUR CHILDREN'S MINISTRY BY YOUR FAITHFUL SERVICE AND LOVE FOR OUR KIDS.

 THANK YOU FOR **RAISIN'** THE STANDARD IN OUR CHILDREN'S MINISTRY BY YOUR FAITHFUL SERVICE AND LOVE FOR OUR KIDS.

 THANK YOU FOR **RAISIN'** THE STANDARD IN OUR CHILDREN'S MINISTRY BY YOUR FAITHFUL SERVICE AND LOVE FOR OUR KIDS.

 THANK YOU FOR **RAISIN'** THE STANDARD IN OUR CHILDREN'S MINISTRY BY YOUR FAITHFUL SERVICE AND LOVE FOR OUR KIDS.

Food

YOU ADD
SO MUCH TO OUR
CHILDREN'S MINISTRY!
THANK YOU FOR BEING
THE SALT OF THE
EARTH AND ROUNDING
OUT OUR TEAM!

YOU ADD
SO MUCH TO OUR
CHILDREN'S MINISTRY!
THANK YOU FOR BEING
THE SALT OF THE
EARTH AND ROUNDING
OUT OUR TEAM!

YOU ADD
SO MUCH TO OUR
CHILDREN'S MINISTRY!
THANK YOU FOR BEING
THE SALT OF THE
EARTH AND ROUNDING
OUT OUR TEAM!

YOU ADD
SO MUCH TO OUR
CHILDREN'S MINISTRY!
THANK YOU FOR BEING
THE SALT OF THE
EARTH AND ROUNDING
OUT OUR TEAM!

Food

God
MUSTARD

had you in mind when we planned our children's program
this year—because you've done a marvelous job of
spicing it up and smothering kids with His love!
Thank you—and enjoy!

God
MUSTARD

had you in mind when we planned our children's program
this year—because you've done a marvelous job of
spicing it up and smothering kids with His love!
Thank you—and enjoy!

God
MUSTARD

had you in mind when we planned our children's program
this year—because you've done a marvelous job of
spicing it up and smothering kids with His love!
Thank you—and enjoy!

God
MUSTARD

had you in mind when we planned our children's program
this year—because you've done a marvelous job of
spicing it up and smothering kids with His love!
Thank you—and enjoy!

Gum

Thanks for your faithful help!

Such faithfulness keeps the programs in our ministry from getting all gummed up!

(And we're delighted to see how creatively you **stick** with it!)

Thanks for your faithful help!

Such faithfulness keeps the programs in our ministry from getting all gummed up!

(And we're delighted to see how creatively you **stick** with it!)

Thanks for your faithful help!

Such faithfulness keeps the programs in our ministry from getting all gummed up!

(And we're delighted to see how creatively you **stick** with it!)

Gum

Thanks for being such a **cool** addition to our Children's Ministry team. No matter how **hot** a situation becomes, your **warm** heart toward each kid is noticed by God and appreciated by others. As you reflect on your contribution, we thought ICE might be nice!

Thanks for being such a **cool** addition to our Children's Ministry team. No matter how **hot** a situation becomes, your **warm** heart toward each kid is noticed by God and appreciated by others. As you reflect on your contribution, we thought ICE might be nice!

Thanks for being such a **cool** addition to our Children's Ministry team. No matter how **hot** a situation becomes, your **warm** heart toward each kid is noticed by God and appreciated by others. As you reflect on your contribution, we thought ICE might be nice!

Thanks for being such a **cool** addition to our Children's Ministry team. No matter how **hot** a situation becomes, your **warm** heart toward each kid is noticed by God and appreciated by others. As you reflect on your contribution, we thought ICE might be nice!

WE'RE **BANDING** TOGETHER FOR THE SPIRITUAL **AID** OF OUR KIDS. THANKS FOR BRINGING A **SOFT** HEART FOR CHILDREN AND A **FLEXIBLE** ATTITUDE THAT **PROTECTS** THOSE IN YOUR CARE!

WE LOVE AND APPRECIATE YOU!

WE'RE **BANDING** TOGETHER FOR THE SPIRITUAL **AID** OF OUR KIDS. THANKS FOR BRINGING A **SOFT** HEART FOR CHILDREN AND A **FLEXIBLE** ATTITUDE THAT **PROTECTS** THOSE IN YOUR CARE!

WE LOVE AND APPRECIATE YOU!

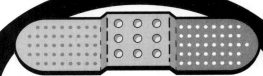

WE'RE **BANDING** TOGETHER FOR THE SPIRITUAL **AID** OF OUR KIDS. THANKS FOR BRINGING A **SOFT** HEART FOR CHILDREN AND A **FLEXIBLE** ATTITUDE THAT **PROTECTS** THOSE IN YOUR CARE!

WE LOVE AND APPRECIATE YOU!

WE'RE **BANDING** TOGETHER FOR THE SPIRITUAL **AID** OF OUR KIDS. THANKS FOR BRINGING A **SOFT** HEART FOR CHILDREN AND A **FLEXIBLE** ATTITUDE THAT **PROTECTS** THOSE IN YOUR CARE!

WE LOVE AND APPRECIATE YOU!

Household Items

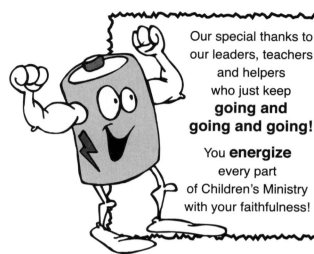

Our special thanks to
our leaders, teachers
and helpers
who just keep
**going and
going and going!**

You **energize**
every part
of Children's Ministry
with your faithfulness!

Our special thanks to
our leaders, teachers
and helpers
who just keep
**going and
going and going!**

You **energize**
every part
of Children's Ministry
with your faithfulness!

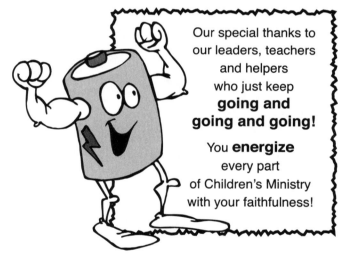

Our special thanks to
our leaders, teachers
and helpers
who just keep
**going and
going and going!**

You **energize**
every part
of Children's Ministry
with your faithfulness!

Our special thanks to
our leaders, teachers
and helpers
who just keep
**going and
going and going!**

You **energize**
every part
of Children's Ministry
with your faithfulness!

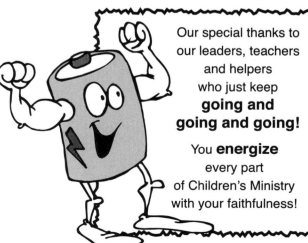

Our special thanks to
our leaders, teachers
and helpers
who just keep
**going and
going and going!**

You **energize**
every part
of Children's Ministry
with your faithfulness!

Our special thanks to
our leaders, teachers
and helpers
who just keep
**going and
going and going!**

You **energize**
every part
of Children's Ministry
with your faithfulness!

Household Items

Thank you

for your commitment to sharing the Book of books with the children of our church—the leaders of tomorrow!

Thank you

for your commitment to sharing the Book of books with the children of our church—the leaders of tomorrow!

Thank you

for your commitment to sharing the Book of books with the children of our church—the leaders of tomorrow!

Thanks for being one more **light** on the path connecting kids with the real meaning of Christmas! May God bless and enrich your holiday season!

Thanks for being one more **light** on the path connecting kids with the real meaning of Christmas! May God bless and enrich your holiday season!

Thanks for being one more **light** on the path connecting kids with the real meaning of Christmas! May God bless and enrich your holiday season!

Thanks for being one more **light** on the path connecting kids with the real meaning of Christmas! May God bless and enrich your holiday season!

Emery Boards

Thanks for choosing to help **smooth out** the rough edges in our Children's Ministry. Your helpful presence **shapes** many young lives!

Thanks for choosing to help **smooth out** the rough edges in our Children's Ministry. Your helpful presence **shapes** many young lives!

Thanks for choosing to help **smooth out** the rough edges in our Children's Ministry. Your helpful presence **shapes** many young lives!

Thanks for choosing to help **smooth out** the rough edges in our Children's Ministry. Your helpful presence **shapes** many young lives!

Thanks for choosing to help **smooth out** the rough edges in our Children's Ministry. Your helpful presence **shapes** many young lives!

Thanks for choosing to help **smooth out** the rough edges in our Children's Ministry. Your helpful presence **shapes** many young lives!

Celebrating with you the coming of Jesus, the **light of the world**. We're delighted to see how **His light** shines through you to bless our kids!

Celebrating with you the coming of Jesus, the **light of the world**. We're delighted to see how **His light** shines through you to bless our kids!

Celebrating with you the coming of Jesus, the **light of the world**. We're delighted to see how **His light** shines through you to bless our kids!

Household Items

Your involvement in Children's Ministry gives new meaning to "Got it Covered!"

Thanks for **covering** your God-given assignment with faithfulness, prayer and joy! We appreciate all you do!

Your involvement in Children's Ministry gives new meaning to "Got it Covered!"

Thanks for **covering** your God-given assignment with faithfulness, prayer and joy! We appreciate all you do!

Your involvement in Children's Ministry gives new meaning to "Got it Covered!"

Thanks for **covering** your God-given assignment with faithfulness, prayer and joy! We appreciate all you do!

Your involvement in Children's Ministry gives new meaning to "Got it Covered!"

Thanks for **covering** your God-given assignment with faithfulness, prayer and joy! We appreciate all you do!

Hand Lotion

Household Items

Softer hands that smell good, too,
Is what this product does for you!
As you rub this lotion on,
Ask God for a heart that's **soft** and **strong**.
Thank Him for His promises, too—
And for the love He'll show through you!

Softer hands that smell good, too,
Is what this product does for you!
As you rub this lotion on,
Ask God for a heart that's **soft** and **strong**.
Thank Him for His promises, too—
And for the love He'll show through you!

Softer hands that smell good, too,
Is what this product does for you!
As you rub this lotion on,
Ask God for a heart that's **soft** and **strong**.
Thank Him for His promises, too—
And for the love He'll show through you!

Household Items

We love the way your Presence in our Program **smoothes out the wrinkles** in our Children's Ministry. Thanks for Being **soft** and **flexible!**

You are appreciated!

We love the way your Presence in our Program **smoothes out the wrinkles** in our Children's Ministry. Thanks for Being **soft** and **flexible!**

You are appreciated!

We love the way your Presence in our Program **smoothes out the wrinkles** in our Children's Ministry. Thanks for Being **soft** and **flexible!**

You are appreciated!

We love the way your Presence in our Program **smoothes out the wrinkles** in our Children's Ministry. Thanks for Being **soft** and **flexible!**

You are appreciated!

We're glad to see how God's love comes through you to our little ones! Children's Ministry takes work—even getting your hands **dirty.** But you are making a difference.

Thank you for sharing your service and His love!

We're glad to see how God's love comes through you to our little ones! Children's Ministry takes work—even getting your hands **dirty.** But you are making a difference.

Thank you for sharing your service and His love!

We're glad to see how God's love comes through you to our little ones! Children's Ministry takes work—even getting your hands **dirty.** But you are making a difference.

Thank you for sharing your service and His love!

We're glad to see how God's love comes through you to our little ones! Children's Ministry takes work—even getting your hands **dirty.** But you are making a difference.

Thank you for sharing your service and His love!

Thanks for **hanging around** with our kids so that your love for our Lord is right where they can see it. Keep **hanging** close to Him. You are appreciated!

Thanks for **hanging around** with our kids so that your love for our Lord is right where they can see it. Keep **hanging** close to Him. You are appreciated!

Thanks for **hanging around** with our kids so that your love for our Lord is right where they can see it. Keep **hanging** close to Him. You are appreciated!

Thanks for **hanging around** with our kids so that your love for our Lord is right where they can see it. Keep **hanging** close to Him. You are appreciated!

Household items

If it weren't for volunteers like you, we'd be **clean** out of wonderful Children's Ministry leaders! Thanks for your **clean**-cut example that teaches so many!

If it weren't for volunteers like you, we'd be **clean** out of wonderful Children's Ministry leaders! Thanks for your **clean**-cut example that teaches so many!

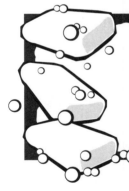

If it weren't for volunteers like you, we'd be **clean** out of wonderful Children's Ministry leaders! Thanks for your **clean**-cut example that teaches so many!

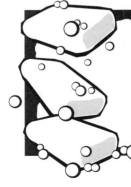

If it weren't for volunteers like you, we'd be **clean** out of wonderful Children's Ministry leaders! Thanks for your **clean**-cut example that teaches so many!

Napkins
(or other small service-related gifts)

Thank you

for being a great example of a servant. You have demonstrated Christlike service to many who watch you. May this small token encourage you as you continue to **serve the Lord** with gladness!

Thank you

for being a great example of a servant. You have demonstrated Christlike service to many who watch you. May this small token encourage you as you continue to **serve the Lord** with gladness!

Thank you

for being a great example of a servant. You have demonstrated Christlike service to many who watch you. May this small token encourage you as you continue to **serve the Lord** with gladness!

Thank you

for being a great example of a servant. You have demonstrated Christlike service to many who watch you. May this small token encourage you as you continue to serve the Lord with gladness!

We're glad to see how God's grace has given you **extra strength** to meet the needs of our kids! We pray you will remain **extra resistant** to distractions and be as **gentle** as a **PUFF** toward each child's needs.

We're glad to see how God's grace has given you **extra strength** to meet the needs of our kids! We pray you will remain **extra resistant** to distractions and be as **gentle** as a **PUFF** toward each child's needs.

We're glad to see how God's grace has given you **extra strength** to meet the needs of our kids! We pray you will remain **extra resistant** to distractions and be as **gentle** as a **PUFF** toward each child's needs.

We're glad to see how God's grace has given you **extra strength** to meet the needs of our kids! We pray you will remain **extra resistant** to distractions and be as **gentle** as a **PUFF** toward each child's needs.

Recipe Cards

Recipe for Effective Children's Ministry at Our Church

Ingredients:

YOU!
God's Word
A bunch of kids
A plan of action

Directions:

Thoroughly mix ingredients together with time and prayer. Bake at temperatures well warmed by love, keeping an eye on how God changes the children's lives. Garnish with laughter and serve to the King as a special gift of love at Christmas.

Recipe for Effective Children's Ministry at Our Church

Ingredients:

YOU!
God's Word
A bunch of kids
A plan of action

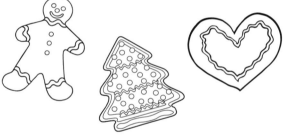

Directions:

Thoroughly mix ingredients together with time and prayer. Bake at temperatures well warmed by love, keeping an eye on how God changes the children's lives. Garnish with laughter and serve to the King as a special gift of love at Christmas.

Recipe for Effective Children's Ministry at Our Church

Ingredients:

YOU!
God's Word
A bunch of kids
A plan of action

Directions:

Thoroughly mix ingredients together with time and prayer. Bake at temperatures well warmed by love, keeping an eye on how God changes the children's lives. Garnish with laughter and serve to the King as a special gift of love at Christmas.

Sponges

Let's be like sponges this year!
Soft and **flexible** in our hearts
Saturated by freely **absorbing** God's Word
Living **clean** in light of His forgiveness
Oozing His love when **squeezed** by the press of life.

We appreciate you!

Let's be like sponges this year!
Soft and **flexible** in our hearts
Saturated by freely **absorbing** God's Word
Living **clean** in light of His forgiveness
Oozing His love when **squeezed** by the press of life.

We appreciate you!

Let's be like sponges this year!
Soft and **flexible** in our hearts
Saturated by freely **absorbing** God's Word
Living **clean** in light of His forgiveness
Oozing His love when **squeezed** by the press of life.

We appreciate you!

WHEN YOU SWISH THIS LITTLE WASHCLOTH OVER YOUR HANDS, WE'D LIKE FOR YOU TO REMEMBER HOW YOUR HELP AND ENCOURAGEMENT HAVE **REFRESHED** OUR ENTIRE CHILDREN'S MINISTRY STAFF THIS YEAR. THANK YOU!

WHEN YOU SWISH THIS LITTLE WASHCLOTH OVER YOUR HANDS, WE'D LIKE FOR YOU TO REMEMBER HOW YOUR HELP AND ENCOURAGEMENT HAVE **REFRESHED** OUR ENTIRE CHILDREN'S MINISTRY STAFF THIS YEAR. THANK YOU!

WHEN YOU SWISH THIS LITTLE WASHCLOTH OVER YOUR HANDS, WE'D LIKE FOR YOU TO REMEMBER HOW YOUR HELP AND ENCOURAGEMENT HAVE **REFRESHED** OUR ENTIRE CHILDREN'S MINISTRY STAFF THIS YEAR. THANK YOU!

WHEN YOU SWISH THIS LITTLE WASHCLOTH OVER YOUR HANDS, WE'D LIKE FOR YOU TO REMEMBER HOW YOUR HELP AND ENCOURAGEMENT HAVE **REFRESHED** OUR ENTIRE CHILDREN'S MINISTRY STAFF THIS YEAR. THANK YOU!

WHEN YOU SWISH THIS LITTLE WASHCLOTH OVER YOUR HANDS, WE'D LIKE FOR YOU TO REMEMBER HOW YOUR HELP AND ENCOURAGEMENT HAVE **REFRESHED** OUR ENTIRE CHILDREN'S MINISTRY STAFF THIS YEAR. THANK YOU!

WHEN YOU SWISH THIS LITTLE WASHCLOTH OVER YOUR HANDS, WE'D LIKE FOR YOU TO REMEMBER HOW YOUR HELP AND ENCOURAGEMENT HAVE **REFRESHED** OUR ENTIRE CHILDREN'S MINISTRY STAFF THIS YEAR. THANK YOU!

On the first Christmas, angels sang to praise God for Jesus' birth. This Christmas, we think you're an angel, too. Thank you for sharing God's love with our children!

On the first Christmas, angels sang to praise God for Jesus' birth. This Christmas, we think you're an angel, too. Thank you for sharing God's love with our children!

On the first Christmas, angels sang to praise God for Jesus' birth. This Christmas, we think you're an angel, too. Thank you for sharing God's love with our children!

On the first Christmas, angels sang to praise God for Jesus' birth. This Christmas, we think you're an angel, too. Thank you for sharing God's love with our children!

Miscellaneous

We can see you've absorbed God's light by the way your life reflects His. Thanks for being like a **star** to our children, showing them the way to Jesus. We appreciate you!

We can see you've absorbed God's light by the way your life reflects His. Thanks for being like a **star** to our children, showing them the way to Jesus. We appreciate you!

We can see you've absorbed God's light by the way your life reflects His. Thanks for being like a **star** to our children, showing them the way to Jesus. We appreciate you!

We can see you've absorbed God's light by the way your life reflects His. Thanks for being like a **star** to our children, showing them the way to Jesus. We appreciate you!

Miscellaneous

May you be enriched by knowing the **key** role you play in the lives of impressionable children. You are being used to **unlock** God's message of love as children share with you their ideas, thoughts and feelings.
Thank you!

May you be enriched by knowing the **key** role you play in the lives of impressionable children. You are being used to **unlock** God's message of love as children share with you their ideas, thoughts and feelings.
Thank you!

May you be enriched by knowing the **key** role you play in the lives of impressionable children. You are being used to **unlock** God's message of love as children share with you their ideas, thoughts and feelings.
Thank you!

May you be enriched by knowing the key role you play in the lives of impressionable children. You are being used to **unlock** God's message of love as children share with you their ideas, thoughts and feelings.
Thank you!

**Postcard of Your City
(attach to message so that
postcard is usable)**

Miscellaneous

Look! It's the place where
you make a difference!

Thank you for serving the Lord
on our Children's Ministry team!

Look! It's the place where
you make a difference!

Thank you for serving the Lord
on our Children's Ministry team!

Look! It's the place where
you make a difference!

Thank you for serving the Lord
on our Children's Ministry team!

Look! It's the place where
you make a difference!

Thank you for serving the Lord
on our Children's Ministry team!

Look! It's the place where
you make a difference!

Thank you for serving the Lord
on our Children's Ministry team!

Look! It's the place where
you make a difference!

Thank you for serving the Lord
on our Children's Ministry team!

Miscellaneous

Thank you for your **smile** and your ministry that will point kids to Jesus. We're glad you've chosen to **stick** with it!

Thank you for your **smile** and your ministry that will point kids to Jesus. We're glad you've chosen to **stick** with it!

Thank you for your **smile** and your ministry that will point kids to Jesus. We're glad you've chosen to **stick** with it!

Thank you for your **smile** and your ministry that will point kids to Jesus. We're glad you've chosen to **stick** with it!

Thank you for your **smile** and your ministry that will point kids to Jesus. We're glad you've chosen to **stick** with it!

Thank you for your **smile** and your ministry that will point kids to Jesus. We're glad you've chosen to **stick** with it!

Blank Name Tags

What's in a **name**? A child's own **name** is the most important word in his or her vocabulary! Thank you for remembering each child's **name** and for giving the individual attention that makes God's amazing love real to a child. We appreciate you!

What's in a **name**? A child's own **name** is the most important word in his or her vocabulary! Thank you for remembering each child's **name** and for giving the individual attention that makes God's amazing love real to a child. We appreciate you!

What's in a **name**? A child's own **name** is the most important word in his or her vocabulary! Thank you for remembering each child's **name** and for giving the individual attention that makes God's amazing love real to a child. We appreciate you!

What's in a **name**? A child's own **name** is the most important word in his or her vocabulary! Thank you for remembering each child's **name** and for giving the individual attention that makes God's amazing love real to a child. We appreciate you!

Office Supplies

Make no mistake about it—God knew yesterday that you'd be here today, making a difference in kids' lives forever! **Erase** any doubt about your mission! His plan, implemented by your love, is making a difference.

Thank you!

Make no mistake about it—God knew yesterday that you'd be here today, making a difference in kids' lives forever! **Erase** any doubt about your mission! His plan, implemented by your love, is making a difference.

Thank you!

Make no mistake about it—God knew yesterday that you'd be here today, making a difference in kids' lives forever! **Erase** any doubt about your mission! His plan, implemented by your love, is making a difference.

Thank you!

Make no mistake about it—God knew yesterday that you'd be here today, making a difference in kids' lives forever! **Erase** any doubt about your mission! His plan, implemented by your love, is making a difference.

Thank you!

Your participation has been a **highlight** in Children's Ministry this year!

Thank you!

Your participation has been a **highlight** in Children's Ministry this year!

Thank you!

Your participation has been a **highlight** in Children's Ministry this year!

Thank you!

Your participation has been a **highlight** in Children's Ministry this year!

Thank you!

Miniature Staplers

We love the way you
hold things together
and *keep* everyone **Connected!**
Thank you for your joyful service in
our Children's Ministry!

We love the way you
hold things together
and *keep* everyone **Connected!**
Thank you for your joyful service in
our Children's Ministry!

We love the way you
hold things together
and *keep* everyone **Connected!**
Thank you for your joyful service in
our Children's Ministry!

We love the way you
hold things together
and *keep* everyone **Connected!**
Thank you for your joyful service in
our Children's Ministry!

We love the way you
hold things together
and *keep* everyone **Connected!**
Thank you for your joyful service in
our Children's Ministry!

We love the way you
hold things together
and *keep* everyone **Connected!**
Thank you for your joyful service in
our Children's Ministry!

Office Supplies

Your ministry with kids is
write on!
Know that you are loved
and appreciated.

Your ministry with kids is
write on!
Know that you are loved
and appreciated.

Your ministry with kids is
write on!
Know that you are loved
and appreciated.

Your ministry with kids is
write on!
Know that you are loved
and appreciated.

Your ministry with kids is
write on!
Know that you are loved
and appreciated.

Your ministry with kids is
write on!
Know that you are loved
and appreciated.

Office Supplies

Office Supplies

Thanks for **sticking** with us through this dynamic season in Children's Ministry. Unlike temporary adhesives, your example, relationships and words will **adhere** to young hearts and minds for eternity!

Thanks for **sticking** with us through this dynamic season in Children's Ministry. Unlike temporary adhesives, your example, relationships and words will **adhere** to young hearts and minds for eternity!

Thanks for **sticking** with us through this dynamic season in Children's Ministry. Unlike temporary adhesives, your example, relationships and words will **adhere** to young hearts and minds for eternity!

Thanks for **sticking** with us through this dynamic season in Children's Ministry. Unlike temporary adhesives, your example, relationships and words will **adhere** to young hearts and minds for eternity!

Scissors
(or scissor-shaped charms)

Your nimble fingers keep our
Children's Ministry on the

Thank you

very much for all you do!

Your nimble fingers keep our
Children's Ministry on the

cutting edge.

Thank you

very much for all you do!

Your nimble fingers keep our
Children's Ministry on the

Thank you

very much for all you do!

Your nimble fingers keep our
Children's Ministry on the

Thank you

very much for all you do!

Team

To make card, photocopy both sides of page onto cardstock, cut to size and fold.

Photos

fold

What do the

ABCs

of Children's Ministry look like at our church?

208

Place Photo Here

THANK YOU!

ABLE **B**EAUTIFUL **C**OMMITTED **D**YNAMIC

ENERGETIC **F**AITHFUL **G**REAT—and more!

Photos

Team

To make card, photocopy both sides of page onto cardstock, cut to size and fold.

✂ - - - -

When there's a job to be done, you look for a team

LIKE THIS!
YOU are the Best!
We're Grateful for you!

Place Photo Here

Volunteers

To make card, photocopy both
sides of page onto cardstock,
cut to size and fold.

This year's **picture** of Children's Ministry

would have been incomplete without you! Thank you for being

clearly focused

on our great God!

Place Photo Here

Index

Note: For an Item Index, please see the Contents Pages.